THE DAY TRADING ILLUSION

A DREAMERS NIGHTMARE

Ken Bednar

Table of Contents

FOREWORD

All prospective day traders fantasize about leading an exciting life day trading from home (or anywhere for that matter), being their own boss and making a lot of money. **This is the "dream".**

As they research day trading, they are bombarded with ads, videos, books and hundreds of websites offering to make them successful and wealthy by day trading. **This is the "illusion".**

About 85% to 90% of these dreamers end up losing all their money. **This is the "nightmare".**

I wrote this book to inform you that you only have about a 10 % chance of making any money if you day trade the stock market. Chances are that you bought a book or some Internet course on day trading to make your dream come true. I am not here to talk you out of your dream. I am here to share information and common experiences that you most likely will not see anywhere else on day trading. In order to make an intelligent informed decision regarding day trading, you should have as much information on the subject as you can.

There are about four to five million day traders in the United States at any given time. They come and they go as they lose all their money. Most come into the game with high expectations and leave frustrated, depressed and with a drained trading account.

As I researched this topic I looked at hundreds of books on day trading. I could not find a single book that explained the ugly truth about the risks and results that most day traders will experience.

Day trading is an abyss. Most day traders get lost and never find their way out as they go from one trading system to another trying to win. If after reading this book you still want to day trade, you do so knowing the possible consequences.

There is nothing wrong with being a dreamer. In fact, dreamers are who made America great. It is great to dream of a better life, but when that dream turns into a nightmare, you better wake up. Please bear in mind that this book was written for anyone day trading or thinking about day trading. There will be experienced traders reading this book as well as people who are just starting to learn about trading. Terminology has to be acceptable to both. Many times it will seem that points are redundant but that is only to emphasize the importance.

CHAPTER 1

DAY TRADING EXPLORED

It is ironic that in order to write a book about "Not Trading", we have to talk about trading. When it comes to day trading, it is all about the time frames, indicators, and the multitude of different trading systems you will use in your quest to be successful. Although the book deals generally with day trading, the fact is that trading in itself and in all time durations is a losing proposition for most traders.

A day trader is usually defined as someone who initiates a trade or several trades in a single day. They usually base their trading decisions off of a smaller time frame chart. The smaller the time frame chart, the more trading opportunities a trader will have. The more trades a trader initiates the more commissions they will pay. Stockbrokers and trading platforms love day traders for this very reason.

The fast pace of the really small time frames like the " 333" tick for example has price printing on a chart extremely fast and trading decisions have to be made in a split second. A trader can be in and out of a trade within minutes. By contrast the 5-minute time frame has price printing on a chart much slower and trading decisions can be thought out to a greater degree. The longer the time frame that is traded, the longer it takes for most setups to materialize. Trading a longer term chart like the 5 or10 minute for example, it is possible to hold a trade most of the day, providing you do not hold the trade overnight. If you do hold overnight this is short term swing trading but can still be classified as "pattern" day trading.

Time frames are tricky and confusing. You can be in a downtrend on the 1-minute chart and in an up trend on the 5-minute chart. If you use two or more time frames in your trading, one can give a buy signal at the same time the other is giving a sell signal.

Most day traders use somewhere between the tick chart and the 10-minute chart for their trading decisions. The shorter the time frame the more trades a trader can make because there are simply more of whatever setups you are looking for to initiate a trade. Some day traders look at two or more time frames. Usually it will be a smaller time frame and a longer time frame. The idea being that you would want to trade the smaller time frame chart in the direction of the longer time frame chart. So now we have a basic idea of what a day trader is. Let's look at why people decide to try this risky business of day trading. Remember that they are falling for an illusion.

Starting a traditional business the right way takes a lot of capital and a lot of work. You will have all kinds of regulations, overhead, taxes, employee concerns, book keeping, and so on. What your looking for is a way to make money with very little start up capital and very little "red tape". You have heard many success stories of people making money in the stock market, so you think day trading is a viable avenue to achieve your dream. All you need is a small amount of money to open a trading account and you are ready to conquer the world of day trading. Seems simple enough.

You are absolutely positive that everyone is making boatloads of money day trading, or else there would not be so many people doing it. There would not be so many books promoting it, and there would not be so many trading firms showing how easy it is over the Internet. After all, there are hundreds of videos on You Tube that will show you how to trade. Maybe you have heard of this disease, it's called "herd mentality".

There are many books written by authors who experience an event. Some write about an experience someone else had. Some take an unpleasant event and exploit it for the sole purpose of making money. Such would be the case for books written about "murder trials, homicides of some fashion, celebrity or sporting accidents, school shootings, bombings, a tragedy, the survival of some sort of disaster", and the list could go on and on.

Many authors write books on personal achievements. Some examples would be successes in "starting some business venture, winning a medal at the Olympics, climbing Mount Everest, excelling in some sport or competition, being an Astronaut, and the list could go on.

Let me ask you some questions. If you were to go to any bookstore and look for a book on why someone should NOT day trade, do you think you will find one? I doubt it. Did you ever see a book, any book, written by a stockbroker, about the success of day trading? I don't think so.

Would it be safe to assume that all brokers would be day-traders if there was any success in it? After all, they are in the business of trading stocks, futures and options. You would be hard pressed to find just one. They know the risks are just too high to make consistent profits day trading. The key word being consistent. Their job is to provide as many ways as possible for you to trade and make a guaranteed commission on each trade you make.

By contrast, you will find hundreds of books on how to day trade the stock market. Now, what are you supposed to think? There are hundreds of books about how to day trade and hardly a single book on why you should not day trade. Why do you think that is?

I decided to write this book to emphasize the massive amount of "failures" connected to day trading. I mainly traded the S&P500 (ES) and NASDAQ (NQ) futures, but also delved into stocks using the NASDAQ Level II screens. Along the way I also traded ETF's, and options. It does not matter, pick your poison. In over 20 years of trading, I have met and known hundreds of day traders. I am going to tell you something that will blow you away. Ready? I don't know of a single trader trading from home that I would consider successful at day trading and almost all lose money on a yearly basis.

Now, floor and institutional traders aside, they are the average day traders enemy because they are the ones taking most of your money. They have access to market information and breaking news before the average trader. Trading the index futures contracts (ES, NQ, YM) is a zero sum game. For every winner there is a loser.

I wrote this book to confront some of the myths of day trading and to open your eyes to the high risks involved. There will of course be those who take exception to this book. Try as they may, they cannot dispute the facts that are brought forth in this book. As a former day trader wanting to help, I felt it was important that you should have input from both sides before day trading your hard earned money.

It is not the purpose of this book to stop anyone from day trading. Many will try day trading anyways. Just remember that I was here to give you the "other" side of the media brainwashing that you see everyday. You make your decision and live with it.

Keep what you learned here in the back of your mind should you decide to try day trading. Chances are about 85 to 90 % that you will wake up one day and realize that the scenarios you read about here in this book are actually taking place in your day trading. You will also realize that if you do not do something about it your results will be the same as described in the book.

This book just covers the tip of the iceberg on the illusion of day trading. The trading scenarios and schemes are endless. If you don't believe what this book has to offer now, chances are very good that you will after you try to day trade.

The financial markets domestically and globally are so complex and intertwined by so many influential factors, that it is way beyond the comprehension of most people. This book barely scratches the surface on some of these.

I just do not want you to embark on this venture with your "eyes wide shut". I wrote this book to help you make an intelligent decision on day trading. Someone had to bring to light the "other" side of the story.

How many times have you ever dreamed of being wealthy? Never having to worry about money for you or your family. You know that you are stuck at your job because of obligations and responsibilities. You see the stock market as a possible avenue to financial freedom. How dangerous can it be? It seems that everyone is doing it. You can do it from home or office so it can't get much more convenient than that. You can even trade from your smart phone.

You see these advertisements all the time in trading magazines:

Quit your day job and day trade for a living.

Day trading is the perfect business, be finished by noon everyday.

Our trading system has 80% accuracy.

What if you could work just 30 to 90 minutes a day and be wealthy.

Learn to trade from a veteran trader of 20 years.

These are but a few of the catch phrases used to shift your thinking from rational to the feeling of being left behind. You see so many of these promotions that you begin to believe that everyone is making money in the market but you. They want you to believe everybody is winning at this game so you better hurry and get in the game. You have now lost the ability to rationalize and think objectively. In your mind you may question the validity of these statements but your curiosity takes over and clouds your judgment.

Just to be clear, I am not talking about investors of mutual funds or long-term stocks. I am talking about index and stock day traders using the eminis, ETF's or NASDAQ Level II screen. The eminis are highly leveraged trading instruments that require only a small amount of capital to get started. Just about anybody with a source of income will have enough money to open a trading account. That is why they are so popular...and so dangerous to your bank account.

I am going to try my best to convince the majority of you that day trading from your home, office or anywhere is a losing proposition. That 85% to 90% of the traders are unsuccessful and most lose all their _initial_ trading capital very quickly. I am not talking about institutional or floor traders, as they have many advantages that home traders do not have. They are the ones that take your money on a consistent basis.

Chances of one being successful at day trading are very remote. Just ask yourself this question. How many day traders do I personally know that make a living day trading from home? Chances are that you don't know a single person, and that should tell you something. If it was easy to make money in the stock market by day trading, don't you think a lot more people would be doing it?

If it was such an easy way to make money everybody would be cashing out their 401k's and getting second mortgages on their houses to trade. Maybe you think that you are smarter than the average person when it comes to day trading. Maybe you think that you are the "little red engine that could". Chances are that you will be derailed financially.

I am going to advise you to save your money, get a good job with a steady income or maybe open up that business you always dreamed of. For those that already have a steady paycheck and consider this a hobby, save it and go on vacation somewhere, buy a boat, motorcycle or hot tub. Just don't give it to the fat cats on Wall Street, investment firms and in the trading pits.

I am going to try to spare you the agony of wasting your life away watching charts all day long thinking that there must be a way to beat these guys. **There is not, for most.** I am trying to spare you the agony of having your emotions stretched to the limits on most days as trade after trade just does not work out like it was supposed to. Make no mistake, your nerves will be tested and like it or not, it may affect your behavior.

After reading this short book, there are those that will still be determined to punish themselves by trying to day trade anyway. They will try, knowing now that they probably will not succeed and end up losing all their money. It is their money to lose or do with as they wish. But if you work hard for your money, why in the world would you want to give it away.

The whole idea of day trading is nothing more than a big charade. They (the professional investment institutions) want you to believe that you can win and make money by day trading. That is why there are so many different ways to trade and why it is so easy. They will stop at nothing to separate you from your money. That is how they make their living.

If you are in the stock market, your money is at risk. I don't care what time frame you are trading. There is always the risk of losing your money if you are exposed to the stock market. It is just that simple.

CHAPTER 2

STUDIES AND REPORTS

There are many studies on day trading available. Do your own research on them. The one thing that they all have in common is that the vast majority of day traders are going to lose most of their money. That is a FACT.

In almost all studies the figures are over 80%. Forbes reported on a North American Securities Administration study that found over 77% of day traders lost money. Many other studies are close to 90%. And for the 10% that were marginally successful, the small amount they made just was not worth it both physically and emotionally. Your "stress" level will be tested on a daily basis and you will notice changes in behavior. Just be aware of them as most will be negative in nature.

There is no difference for losing day traders in other countries. Business Week reported that a co-study by the University of California and University of Taipei found that 82% of day traders were losers.

Out of 925,000 traders in the study of the Taiwan Stock Exchange, 750,000 were losers. The losers averaged $45 per day. That means they lost an average of $11,00 a year.

This study is over 10 years old, which means with the advent of more online day traders; this figure could be up exponentially. With more people thinking they can be wealthy by day trading from home, this figure could be as high as 90% losers. Potential day traders are in and out of the market and lose their initial starting capital so fast; it is almost impossible to get accurate numbers.

But here is the real kicker. The winners averaged only about $62,000 a year (before taxes) for all their risk taking and emotional roller coaster rides. That is only slightly better than the average pay in the United States, which is $50,000 per year. Those people get a steady paycheck while the day trader has no idea when or if he will get paid.

Another study is by Ronald L Johnson for the NASAA. Johnson concluded in "An Analysis of Public Day Trading at a Retail Day Trading Firm (8/9/99) " that the majority of traders lost money and a vast majority ran the risk of losing every penny in their account.

Maybe you are the 5% or 10 % making a little money day trading, good for you. You are the minority. But readers need to be reminded that if a trader is successful, it is their money they are taking. Somebody has to lose for someone else to win.

Another report on day trading is Senate Report 106-364. This is a matter of public record for anyone to research and read. They held hearings and reported that _more than_ 75% of day traders lost most or all of their initial trading capital.

In trading firm surveys by the Senate Subcommittee, one trading firm testified that only about 20% of their day trading clients made any profit at all. Their average client quit trading after 1 month and lost an average of $50,000.

Another trading firm testified that if day traders that trade from home are included in the results, that fewer than 10% will ever show a profit.

In review of the reports and testimonies given to the Senate Subcommittee, the _**fact**_ is that 75% -90% of new day traders go bust or quit trading within a month of placing their first trade.

Look at some of the trading blog threads. As soon as someone posts that they think day trading is a losing game, there are numerous posts from all these successful day traders claiming that person just was not smart enough to beat the market at day-trading. Let the facts speak for themselves.

Do your own research. See if you can find a truly successful day-trader in your trading circle. Expand your horizon and try to find a successful day-trader anywhere, in person. Remember this, a truly successful trader is making "consistent" profits every year.

Theoretically, anyone with a college degree or trade skill can make around $50,000 a year (every year) in the job market. This is the average wage in the US as of 2012. If you cannot make at least as much as you would actually working and drawing a paycheck, you are not successful. Twist it any way you want to make yourself feel better. That is human nature. If you think making a few hundred or thousand dollars a year makes you successful, you are wasting your time and life looking at charts all day long. You are cheating your family and yourself out of precious time here on earth. I just hope you realize it before it is too late.

Almost all time proven trading millionaires and billionaires are longer time frame investors, not day traders. They recognize an opportunity in a particular stock or mutual fund and they buy and hold that security. This method is among the best to make money in the stock market unless you actively watch the market and swing trade long term. A trader has a better chance to turn a profit by swing trading longer time frames than by day trading. At least you would be trading within an established trend. You would be in a trade for weeks to months.

The problem is that day traders want "instant" gratification. They want to make money and get closure everyday. They like the fast action. They want to know where they stand everyday. They think safe mutual funds are to slow. They become an income stream for Wall Street.

CHAPTER 3

THE LURE OF DAY TRADING

The lure of day trading is analogous to the Greek Mythology of the Sirens who sang beautiful songs and lured sailors to their demise on the rocks. They preyed on their wants and desires to give them a false sense of serenity and security. The stock market is singing, and with a single click of your mouse you could make all your wants, desires and dreams come true. An unlimited amount of money is at your beckon call. All the things you ever wanted to buy, but could not afford, could be yours. Where else do you have this kind of power and need so little cash to play the game?

Because you only need a small amount of cash to day trade the index eminis compared to stocks (as of this writing), it is very poplar with day traders. The action is fast paced and the possibility to make a lot of money in minutes or hours lures traders like fish to a minnow on a hook. Let's look at the minis. For about a $5000 cash balance you could open an account and trade 3 S&P emini contracts that will give you $150 for every point you make. Twenty points will yield you $3000. That is 60% on your money. How's that for instant money in a single day? On a trend day it is possible. But on average there is only about 2 trend days a month and they are usually half over before anyone figures it out. On top of that, almost everyone will exit the trade early and only catch a very small percentage of the big move. Even when the market lets you win it limits you to peanuts, but it sure makes you want to try again. Yes, you got them right where they want you.

By contrast, if you wanted to day trade stocks you would need about $25,000 to open and trade an account and be a "Pattern Day Trader". **Pattern Day Trader** is a term defined by the U.S. Securities and Exchange Commission to describe a stock market trader as someone who executes 4 (or more) day trades in 5 business days in a margin account. As the trader is exposed to the dangers of day trading and intraday risks and potential rewards, they are subject to specific requirements and restrictions.

A non-pattern day trader can still place day trades but the total must be 3 or less in a 5-day period. Realistically, how many shares can you effectively purchase with a small account?

They (the trading establishment) want you to believe that you could do all this from the comfort of your home. What could be easier? It must be easy to make money day trading because there are so many traders selling winning trading systems and computer programs to help me be successful. I just can't figure out why everybody is not doing it.

There it is right in front of you on your computer. The means to make hundreds or thousands of dollars daily is at your fingertips. Think about it. Where else could you have an opportunity like this? You could trade from home, a coffee shop, the beach or anywhere in the world. You call the shots. You are your own boss and you only need about $5000 to start. All you have to do is what millions of other traders have not been able to do, beat the stock market on a consistent basis.

Oh sure, every trader has a good run here and there. But they always, without exception, come to an end. Quitting the game IF you are lucky enough to be ahead is the only way to walk away and be a winner. But guess what, that almost never happens. We humans are by nature greedy, some more than others. But the gamblers day-trading the market are on the high end of that greedy list, or they would not be trading at all.

The one trait that will doom most traders is PRIDE. They are confident that they can beat the market at day trading. They are convinced that they can find a way. All they need is the right combinations of trading indicators or the right system. They do not realize that all indicators are just different types of bait and lures. What works this week may not work next week. Just like a fish changes his preferences, so does the market.

The market changes and those great indicators do not work anymore. How could that be? You back tested them over many months. The market will let you win enough trades just to keep you on the hook. They want you to think you can win big by day trading. It is the perfect scam and it is all legal.

I know, you think all you need is a little more time to perfect your trading system. You have not yet realized that it is impossible to perfect any trading system. It simply does not exist. Most, if not all, will be buying a trading system from another trader on the Internet. Who by the way is also most likely a loser at day trading. For only a few hundred dollars to several thousand dollars these guys will "guarantee" that you will win if you use their system. Run away from any guarantees. No one can guarantee you will win in the stock market anymore than they can guarantee you can win big in Las Vegas.

Or better yet, if you give this other guy, $300 a month, he will send you trading signals. That sounds better because you don't have to learn anything this way. Just do what this "highly experienced professional trader" wants me to do each day. If he can keep you on the line for 4 or 5 months then he made his $1500 off of you. After you do not win, chances are that you will move on to another winning trading system. I hope you can tell when I am being facetious in this book.

But wait, you say, I am not going to cheap out. I know that you only get what you pay for in this world. Therefore it stands to reason that if I spend thousands of dollars on a computer program for trading that I will be way better off than buying those cheaper systems. Most of the time that is true, but not this time. Usually the seller is just that, a computer programmer and not a winning trader. The seller just wants you to believe you are getting something "special", and plays to your desperation.

After all the fancy colorful lines, arrows and dots, it is still just a simple computer program using indicators that everyone in the world has. By the way, do not ever get duped into believing that they have some proprietary trading indicator that you just have to have. I cannot stress this enough, ALL INDICATORS ARE LAGGING. They only tell you what has already happened, not what will happen in the future with any certainty.

I do not know anyone that got to be a millionaire by day trading. Long Term trading, yes I know of a few. The Wall Street money machine wants all traders to believe that the fastest way to wealth is by day trading. By getting hot tips, actively trading, and using any of the thousands of useless indicators and strategies is the golden path to prosperity. Take special note that it is your brokers golden path because he makes money on every trade you put on whether you win or lose. It is your path to financial ruin.

Sure most day-traders get lucky once in a while. A blind squirrel finds a nut every now and then too. But that blind squirrel will eventually run out of luck and so will you.

Las Vegas has the same kind of lure as day trading. Just because you go to Las Vegas one time and hit a jackpot, does not make you a good slot machine player, you got lucky, plain and simple. If you quit and never go back, you beat them. But if you keep going back, you will eventually give them all your winnings and then some. It's the law of percentages, and it holds true with the day trading.

But wait you say. If I just pull a handle on a slot machine, I know there is no skill involved and I am at the mercy of mother luck. There is no thinking or analyzing on my part. But with trading I can look at past data and charts and apply as many indicators as I want to find a trade I like. I can minimize or even eliminate luck from my equation. I keep reminding you that charts only tell you where you have been. They do not tell you where you are going. We just make up stuff, call it an indicator, apply it to a chart and hope we are right.

When you pull the handle on a slot machine, it is exactly like placing a day-trade on the eminis or on a stock. Instead of being at the mercy of the machine, you are at the mercy of the market and market makers. Sure, you looked at your lagging indicators and gave it your best informed guess based on what the indicator did before on past charts. You see, everything has to do with the past. How does that help you when you need to know the future?

But the bottom line is that no trader sitting at home behind a desk knows what the market will definitely do as far as direction and price run. There are just to many variables in this new global economy. Institutional super computers will run the market up and down for their benefit.

The trading community does not like to be compared to gambling. The average person has a negative view and opinion of gambling and they do not want that to be associated with day trading. Gambling is a highly regulated activity, but regulations vary from state to state. The owner of the casino, otherwise known as "the house" knows beyond any doubt that at the end of the day, he will make money. In the long run it is almost impossible to beat the house. The odds are in their favor and stacked against the player.

Lets take a roulette wheel for example. You would believe that you have a 50% chance of winning because there are equal numbers of RED and BLACK slots. But because there are two green slots or two zero slots, that drops your percentage down to 48% winning odds. The house gets 52% winning odds. Over the long run, who would eventually win? The same holds true with day trading as the institutional traders and market makers are the house.

I want to emphasize over and over that the purpose of this book is not to discourage anyone from day trading. I am writing this book to bring your attention to the almost impossible task ahead of you if you should decide to day trade. I am in no way saying that you could not be successful day trading, only that it would be the same as swimming the English Channel surrounded by sharks if you should decide to do so. We just have sharks of a different nature here trading with us.

I don't care what you heard, read or what anyone has told you about day trading The fact is that being able to day trade for a living is so remote that no one can put figures to the probabilities. It is impossible to determine how many average home traders, if any, trade successfully for a living. The Internal Revenue Service might be able to determine how many traders write off losses or make profits every year. But to my knowledge they do not release these figures.

There are no census, polls or surveys that are done every year or two. Also, you would never get an accurate and honest response if there were. Traders do not like to admit that they are in the group of losers. They will declare that they are winners to their last breath.

Most authors do extensive research, collect data and then write their book. In this case there is not much true honest research about the success of day trading from the public sector. A trading firm would have all the trades placed with them by day traders. It is safe to assume that they all compile data on day trades placed. Since the report would show that the majority would be losing trades, they would not want that information to get out to the public. You will not see any day trading performance reports published by any trading institutions.

Remember that I am talking about day trading stocks and the eminis, and not talking about buying a particular stock and holding it for a longer specified period. Other than the fact that you should have about $50,000 in your trading account to trade stocks, there is nothing wrong with researching and buying a company stock that you think will go up. Just remember that it will only go up if demand for that stock increases. That almost always means that institutional buying is needed for the stock to rise. Are you starting to see the BIG picture here? You as a trader are always dependent on other traders and factors. As much as you want to be in control, you are not.

The stock Market is probably the greatest scam and Ponzi scheme ever designed by the human race. Coming in at a close second would be the Insurance Industry. A stock depends on fresh money coming in to drive the price up. Just like a Ponzi scheme, those that bought at the bottom probably made money, while those that bought near the top will never see a profit as the price of the stock falls from those ridiculous levels.

Remember, you are buying nothing more than a piece of paper. Just ask all the General Motors shareholders who lost every cent when they went into bankruptcy, and came out a different car company.

Apple stock went from $30 to over $700 just because they came out with a few phones and gadgets. Are you kidding me? This was mostly fund and pension managers driving the price up to just ridiculous levels. This reminds me of the trotter horse trainers who used to hold a carrot in front of the horse to make him go around the track. That stupid horse would just keep chasing that carrot, but never catching it. Well, every so often these high tech companies change a few things on their latest and greatest and hold it in front of the people who just have to have it. And even though they just bought the best last month, their next carrot is waiting.

Let's get back to the day trading. Now, take the fact that you only need about $1100 margin to day trade one emini contract and you can see the "LURE". Yes, fisherman know what a lure is. What kind of fish are you? Keep in mind that you may need more cash ($2500 to $5000) to initially open an account.

I know that no matter what anyone tells you, some of you reading this book, will still give day-trading a try. Be prepared to have every emotion tested and get used to being disappointed. Some realize it sooner than others. Most do not last a year before they exhaust their account. It makes sense. It is like a football team offense telling the opposite team defense, the exact plays they are going to run, and expect to win the game. Every trader on the planet watches support and resistance levels. Remind me again how that gives you an advantage over everyone else.

There are many trials and tribulations that you will go through before you are convinced. You will trade endless winning systems and configurations in many different time frames. You will trade all kinds of different charts from "tick" to different "minute" intervals. You will tinker and change all the settings on your indicators hoping to find the "magic" numbers that give the edge. Of course if you run out of money first, you won't get this far.

There will be many times when you think you have it all figured out. You will just need a tweak here and a tweak there. Reminds me of the smoker who could quit any time he wants because he has done it a hundred times before.

You will think the market is psychic because it always seemed to figure out all of your tweaks. You will be convinced the market is out to get you because it seems that every other trader you came across on the trading blogs or trading rooms is making boatloads of money everyday. You are just hoping the market does not run out of money before you can get your boatload.

The S&P emini is by far the most popular emini to trade, so I refer to that trading vehicle often. It is traded world wide almost 24 hours a day by institutions and retail traders alike. It has the most liquidity as it trades approximately 800,000 contracts in a single day as of this writing.

On one hand we have large institutional professional traders with multiple super computers running complex algorithms that actually get informational data BEFORE all home traders. And on the other hand we have Mr. average day trader who read a few books and maybe was swayed into buying a trading system or two on the Internet, and trades from a Dell or HP laptop at home.

Does that sound fair to you? How can the average trader from home or office expect to compete?

Day trading is gambling. Day trading is an addiction, but it doesn't appear that way. It fools you into thinking that you are in control of your decisions. You are NOT. They (the market makers) can control you with a simple move of the market....up.....or down. Like all gambling there will be some winners, but there will be many more losers. Think about it. Could the lottery survive if everyone won? Could Las Vegas survive if everyone won? Could the stock market survive if everyone won?

Sometimes you have to just step back and look at everything objectively, instead of with tunnel vision. Most day traders are looking at the stock market with their "eyes wide shut".

Have you used any of these common excuses?

1) If I only stuck to my discipline, I would not have taken the loss.

2) I am learning something with every loss. Believe me, you will be learning something for the rest of your trading career. You will learn to be a very good loser.

3) Every business owner loses money at the start, that's normal. Really? Business owners don't invest on margin. Maximizing margin will destroy a traders account faster than a category 5 hurricane.

4) I just need a little more time. I am so close to perfecting my trading system. Pretty soon everything is going to click. But it never does, the market is ever changing.

5) It takes years of experience to be a good trader, just like anything else. Really? Golfers play the game of golf for years, if not a lifetime, and most never get good at it. Most will never be par golfers no matter how long they play and practice. If you take 100 professional golfers that all started at the same time, someone is first and someone is last. If you take 100 doctors that graduate, yep, someone is first and someone is last. You don't want to go to that doctor who finished last in the class.

Each persons potential is different. Each person can only be as good as their given abilities. Experience is just a word that relates or refers to time and has nothing at all to do with how proficient a person may be. And that goes for any profession. Think about it for a minute. Who would you rather have operate on you? A doctor with 20 years experience, but has been sued 20 times for malpractice, or a doctor who graduated at the top of his or her class with only 5 years experience? Who do you trust more, a politician with 25 years experience gouging the public or a newly elected politician?

The point is simply that the person makes the experience valuable. The experience does not make the person valuable.

I speak of the market as a living, breathing entity. As some dreadful thing that you have to get up and face on a daily basis. If you trade long enough, you will see it this way to. It is your enemy that you must defeat every day. It sees you sitting there in front of your computer and knows that you are interested in day trading. It also knows that you have money to play the game and it is just a matter of time before it gets it all. The market is very patient, traders are not.

There are thousands of trading systems out there. Each one will show you HOW to trade their way. That is all they can do. They can't teach you to win and they can't guarantee you anything. I am going to ask a simple question. Why do you think there are thousands of trading systems out there for sale? Think about it. Are you gullible enough to actually think that every one of them is a winning system? Wouldn't just one winning system be all we need?

You will see hundreds of trading sites and videos of systems beating the market with winning trades. I can guarantee you that they are cherry picking the winners and not showing you the losers. Why would they, it would be bad for business. They are trying to lure you in by painting an illusion in your mind that everyone is making money except you because you are not trading their system. If you are on their website looking to buy a trading system, then they know that you are vulnerable. You have not been successful and you are desperate to prove that you can trade. You want to be a winner.

Keep in mind that most of the videos and trades you will see are hypothetical in nature. That means that those trades were never taken in real time or with real money. Some sites might show you their actual trades. Remember this, they optimize their trades to show the most profit and least losses. Chances are that you as a follower will never duplicate their success. You will always be a dollar short and an hour late.

Also, it is easier to win on a Trading simulator because you have nothing to lose. When you trade with your own money, it is a completely different ballgame. You will not be so care free with your actual money and your decisions will not be as reckless. You will experience this for yourself should you decide to day trade anyway.

CHAPTER 4

MARKET MOVERS

I know that this is a day trading book, but it is important to know and understand what moves the market, even on a day trading level.

Ever wonder why a big trading firm like Goldman Sachs consistently wins more than they lose, while the average trader consistently loses more than they win? In the first quarter of 2010, they did not have a single losing day. Not one. Do you understand the significance of this?

How could this be when the rest of us traders are struggling to put together 2 winning days in a row? Out of 63 trading days in the last quarter of 2011, Goldman Sachs only lost on 17 of those days. They only had 54 losing days in the entire year of 2011. How would you like to have that record? And how small were the losses?

How do they do it? Do they have SUPER traders working there? NO, but they have super computers working there. They run very sophisticated algorithms that let them do everything from skim a quarter point to actually moving the market several points.

No trader, regardless of status, can be right every single time. Obviously, the Goldman traders are right more than they are wrong and they win more than they lose on a consistent basis. Consistent wins is the "keyword" that defines a successful trader. Any trader or trading system can have a several month run, but how did they do for the year, or last several years?

There are very few consistently winning day traders. In most trading circles, almost all of the day traders lose money over time. Why? Because you are trading against the super computers of the big banks and trading firms. Like Vegas, they are the house. Did you know that over 80% of all day trades are done by computers? Most of those trades are done by big institutions. It is like playing chess against IBM's Big Blue.

Speaking of Big Blue and Super Computers, a fairly recent maneuver in the trading world is called HFT Trading. This stands for High Frequency Trading. These are done by big investment banks and institutions.

These programs monitor the market constantly checking prices, volume and so on thousands of times per minute.

Some of these programs are so sophisticated that they initiate trading activity without human intervention.

Other than being super fast, the programs take advantage of a loophole in regulations that obscures part of their activity.

Specifically, the programs can initiate and withdraw thousands of trades at multiple price points almost instantly.

What the programs learn from this activity is where the upper buy range and lower sell range is for any security.

Once the programs know how much the market is willing to pay for a security (the upper limit), they begin selling just below that number.

For example, if you are willing to pay $60 per share for a stock and the current market price is $59, you will probably get your order filled at or very close to $59.

However, if the high frequency programs detect your limit is $60 by flooding the market with orders (and withdrawing them just as fast), the programs will then offer the security at $59.99 or so (but under your $60 limit).

The result is you may pay more to fill your order than you would have under normal circumstances.

This is a very simple example of a very complex activity, but you should know that in addition to costing you money when you buy or sell, these programs could accelerate prices up or down.

What is High Frequency Trading Again?

A High Frequency Trading (or HFT) system is an extremely high-speed computerized trading network designed to literally trade millions of times per minute with the sole purpose of trimming very small fractions of a share price off some stock, ETF or other security off to the owner of the system.

Some refer to this system of trading as "nanotrading". On December 22nd, 1998 the Securities and Exchange Commission enacted the Regulation of Exchanges and Alternative trading Systems and changed the world of trading forever. Very simply the attacking institution bombards a stock with low bids to create downward pressure and artificially drive the price of the stock down. When price retraces they then take a position in the discounted stock. Once they stop the low bids the price rebounds and they take profits. This usually happens very fast and is all transacted by computer networks.

HFT's play a large role in the increase in death-defying plunges (think May 6th, 2010 "flash crash", and Apple's single day plunge) and extreme volatility witnessed in the financial markets as a whole in recent years.

SEC Chairman Mary Schapiro was quoted on September 22, 2010 saying:

" high frequency trading firms have a tremendous capacity to affect the stability and integrity of the equity markets. Currently, however, high frequency trading firms are subject to very little in the way of obligations either to protect that stability by promoting reasonable price continuity in tough times, or to refrain from exacerbating price volatility."

That was another way of saying that they are free to run roughshod over you and me without any repercussions.

Why should you care about HFT's anyway?

You should care because you might be day trading a stock that they are manipulating, and never even know it. You should care because they ultimately take money from you - on the smallest monetary scale while trading.

These techniques are just another weapon that the Professional traders use to profit by trimming off your money on a regular basis. HFT's accounts for 70% of all equity trading volume in all US-based markets - that number is in the hundreds of billions of dollars each day. As of this writing, HTF's are being investigated and there may or may not be changes made.

I use Goldman Sachs here as an example, but there are other big players on Wall Street. The point here is that you have the deck stacked against you right off the bat. You must know and realize that before you place your first trade.

Where do you think the money they make comes from? That's right.......you.

It is important for you to realize and understand that the markets are now manipulated and influenced by bankers, the Federal Reserve, Europe, government statistics that are released and just about any other news that they want to use as an excuse.

How many times has the market received good news and is up say 100 points at the open, only to sell off the rest of the day. How many times has the market received bad news and opened down 100 points only to rally the rest of the day. There is no rhyme or reason why this happens, only to say that the market makers will move the market in the direction they have to in order to make money.

How many times have you entered a trade, watched it move in your direction, and then out of the blue you get a long bar that stops you out. Since most traders put their stops in a tick above or below the last swing high or low, these long bars usually stop you out. After they clear out a lot of the positions by the day traders, the market then resumes the trend direction that you were in. They just don't want you in the trade. They know that if you just got stopped out of a trade and lost money, that very few traders have the experience and emotions to get right back in another trade. They are gun shy.

This is all done by design. It is just one of the many, many ways they have to separate you from your money. It is their job to take money from the masses or else they could not survive.

Over-thinking and emotions are your worst enemies. You must systematically control them in order to have even a remote chance to succeed. Most traders cannot, and then bad trading decisions are made. It is not your fault. Traders are conditioned by the stock market moves to keep them confused and always guessing.

Wait just a minute you say. You heard that you must absolve yourself of all emotions in order to successfully trade. You must enter without question when your trading system signals a trade. And you must exit in the same manner without regard to any market conditions. If you think you can do that, you would not be human.

But wait you say. I have a computer program that will take all the emotion out of the equation. It will get me in and out of a trade automatically. After all, that is what the big banks and trading firms are using. I can be like them right?

The difference is that they have the very best traders and programmers using several sophisticated algorithms in super computers to guide them. They can and do actually move the market with high amounts of volume and leverage that only big institutions have access to. They also have access to information long before you do, and information moves the market.

You have a simple program running on your laptop that uses some moving average cross, a derivative of price action indicator, or any combination of the hundreds of after the fact lagging indicators to make your trading decision for you. Or put another way, they are driving around the racetrack in a Ferrari and you have a Mini Cooper. Clear it up any?

That being said, there are many outside factors that can influence the market and your computer program does not figure them into its equations. Since this is mostly a day trading book, I will just briefly cover some of them here.

There is no entity that has more influence over the stock market than the Federal Reserve. One of the big events is the FOMC meeting by the Federal Reserve Chairman. He has the power to move the markets all by himself. He sets the tone for the direction of the overall market with every meeting he has. He has the ability to raise or lower interest rates. He has the ability to print money. He has the ability to prop the market up, or let the market fall. The general rule is that when interest rates are on the rise, it puts a damper on the equities market. The opposite is true of falling interest rates.

By keeping interest rates low, the chairman is forcing investors out of CD's, bonds and bank savings accounts, and into the stock market, if they want to get any return on their money. Almost all mutual fund managers are investors. He or she is forcing them to take a risk, or make nothing on their money.

The Federal Reserve Chairman can also print money out of thin air with no regard to consequences. He can then use this new money to prop up the stock market under the disguise of "stimulus", "tarp", "twist", or any of the many other programs they devise.

Now we have an inflation or deflation debate, which we will not get into here. Either way, it is not healthy for the economy or the country because the taxpayers always have to pay for it. One fact that there is no debate on, is that each time the Fed cranks up the printing presses and prints billions of dollars that is not backed by anything except empty promises, it devalues the dollar. The dollar becomes worth less. There is not a fiat money system in history that has not failed eventually. The US will eventually have a "reverse split" under new currency.

I recommend you research the Federal Reserve for yourself, but here are some highlights.

What is The Federal Reserve?

You would think by their name that they were a department of the Federal Government. **They are NOT.** The Federal Reserve is actually a privately owned corporation, owned by a secret group of international bankers. They are a private banking cartel that has a total monopoly on "creating" money for the U.S. Government.

At their request our government prints money and gives it to them. Our government then "borrows" the money that they just gave them and pays interest on it. This brings a whole new meaning to the saying " The fastest way to get wealthy is to use other peoples money".

The FED does not actually print money. The Bureau of Engraving and Printing (BEP) print all currency. The Fed is just the master distributor of the money, which they just created.

What do they do?

Most people have no idea at all what the FED is and what they do. Some will say they think the Fed is an agency of the U.S. government and they control the money supply to help the country. That would be completely wrong. Their objective is to make money for the corporation. That's it!

They manipulate interest rates to create "up-down" cycles which always work out to the advantage of the "insiders" as they know exactly when our economy will rise and when it will decline. Think Conspiracy Theory.

Accordingly, ever since the Federal Reserve Act of 1913 was signed into law, when the U.S. Government needs money, they borrow the money from the Federal Reserve.

Now here you go, when the government cannot repay the debt, they create more Federal Reserve Notes so they can loan more to the government (exchange for U.S. bonds) in order to pay off the debt, thereby making the national debt even larger. If this looks like a vicious circle to you, that's because it is.

They have been responsible for every inflationary period and every economic recession that has occurred during their entire unconstitutional existence.

The Federal Reserve does not answer to Congress or the President of the United States. They cannot be audited and are not accountable to any agency or department.

Most Fed policies affect the longer term trading decisions. There is a saying "do not fight the fed". That means that when they want the market to go up, it will go up. When they want the market to go down, it will go down.

The Federal Reserve is a rogue entity. There are a few lawmakers who understand the threat but the rest of the 535 Congressmen and Senators are not smart or brave enough to tackle the "High Society" problem.

CHAPTER 5

THE INDICATOR FALLACY

Ah yes, all those magical technical analysis indicators. Those trend lines that cross, colored dots and arrows at highs and lows, Fibonacci retracement levels, Elliott Wave counts and whatever else we use to try to predict the market. These are the things that all traders are constantly searching for to give them an edge on other traders. They are looking for that "special " indicator that will make them successful and wealthy. It does not exist.

Here is a fact. Indicators work only about 50% of the time in real trading. You may as well toss a coin, throw a dart or just guess at the outcome. Technical Indicators are all illusions or day traders would see them for what they really are. Useless. And guess what? Most of them really only tell you when to enter a trade. There is so mush emphasis on where to get in a trade that traders forget about where they should get out. It is up to you to set your stops and decide when to exit. And here is where the battle is lost because human emotions, thinking, and greed take over.

As if that was not enough stacked against you, remember that you are already at about a 50% success rate. It is simply hit and miss when it comes to any indicator. The market is counting on you to make mistakes. If you get lucky and make a few good trades by making just one mistake you could wipe out all your trading profits. This scenario happens over and over again.

There are so many indicators out there that I cannot list them all here. They all just simply express market movement in as many different forms as the imagination will allow. I am going to put all indicators in the same category. That category would be "useless". Therefore this section will not delve into each indicator, but will instead lump some of the most popular all together.

There may be hundreds or maybe even thousands of different indicators to show what the market has already done. They react after price has already printed. Who cares what it did in the past, I want to know where it is going in the future. Show me an indicator that will show where price is going in the next half hour with at least 90% accuracy. That is what you would need to win at this game.

Let's look briefly at two of the most popular indicators, the MACD and the Moving Average as examples.

Most indicators are derived from "PRICE" action in some way, shape or form. That is because price action is all they have to go on. Since they must wait for price to move in a certain direction before they can give a trading signal, ***they are lagging indicators***, not leading indicators.

You see, there are no real leading indicators despite what anyone tells you or what you read. Most indicators are looking BACK on previous data (could be price or something else) and deriving a conclusion that what happened then will happen now. They are simply hoping that history repeats itself. It has to be this way because it is impossible to look FORWORD at data that has not occurred or printed yet. All they do is project a possible outcome based on previous outcomes. That might work in a world of constants, but we live in a world of variables.

History might repeat itself, but it will not repeat itself every single time and will not repeat EXACTLY as it did before. And that makes it all the more difficult to identify and trade. That is how the market functions and is why we keep making the same mistakes when trying to trade. We keep doing the same things and expect the same results each and every time.

Let's say you notice an MACD line or some Moving Average Line cross up and the market follows up for several points. Then you see it cross down and the market goes down several points. You back test this action over several weeks and say to yourself, I think I found something here that will make me money. You are so excited that you think you have discovered an easy way to make money in the market. You actually start dreaming of all the money you can make and the things you can buy. It is so obvious and it is right in front of you on the charts. See, there you go, looking BACK again.

You never stop to think and ask yourself the obvious question. Why isn't everyone trading this way and making boatloads of money. You simply can't understand how something this simple and obvious could lose money. Your eyes are wide shut.

Remember what I said earlier. Indicators are good at getting you in a trade, but terrible at getting you out with a profit. So it is up to you to decide where to place your stops and exit point. Also remember that an indicator line will sometimes continue in a direction for a while after price has reversed against you. So if your exit is a cross back in the opposite direction, you could very well give up any profits and even incur a loss on the trade.

The MACD and Moving Average are two of the most popular indicators. Which is not always a good thing. Traders also watch for a divergence between price and the indicator. When they see divergence it is supposed to mean that price is going to reverse. This is the whole theory behind divergence. The problem is, that you can find just as many instances where price goes flat or actually continues against the divergence. Divergence only works about half of the time on short time frame day trading charts.

Look over some charts in the tick and one or two minute time frames to observe this for yourself.

Do not think that it only occurs in the lower time frames. It happens more frequently in these time frames because the lower the time frame, the more volatility you have. The more volatility, the more waves price and the indicators will make on the chart.

When an oscillator or moving average line crosses over, these are trading signals. They are supposed to signal some sort of trend change and you as a trader are supposed to jump on for big profits. The truth is that they just bounce around in relation to price movement. They just follow price. **They are reactive, not proactive.**

Many of these indicators work very well on Weekly and Monthly time frames. They are not reliable by themselves, but can be traded along with other market movers for long term only. Trading on a longer time frame will give you a better chance for success but there are no guarantees with any indicator.

All of these different Oscillators and Moving Average crosses work great in a trending market, but the market does not always trend. It usually only trends a few days a month. Most of the time the market moves sideways or consolidates. On chop days these cross over indicators will whipsaw you in and out of trades and whittle your trading account down to nothing. These are the days you dread the most and you do not realize you are in them until you have already lost a few trades.

These are just typical indicators in the sense that they are not reliable. An indicators alternate purpose is to justify a reason that you lost money on a trade. Hey, it wasn't your fault that you lost that trade, you did what you were supposed to do, right? I can't say it enough.

Indicators depend on data and all indicators are lagging. If your whole trading strategy is based on indicators, you are destined to fail.

That is not to say that if you just use "price" only as your trading guide that you will do any better. You will not. Although there are many day trading systems out there that use price movement only for their trading signals, they do not fare better than any other trading system. As an example trading candlestick price bars with all the different Chinese names associated with them will still drain your trading account.

Maybe you figure that you need additional indicators to help you make a trading decision because just one or two is not reliable enough. You are convinced that it will make a big difference in the way you trade because more is better. It doesn't matter which one, just pick one. But what you will find instead is that many times they just contradict each other and confuse you. Many points go by before an entry confirmation is given for you to enter a trade and by that time it is usually to late.

The ways to lose money day trading the market are virtually endless. Traders will try just about anything as a potential trading signal or trading system. Type, "day trading" in your search engine, and look at all the off the wall catch phrase names that are used to get your attention. As much as I would like you to laugh at them, I can't mention them here due to legal ramifications.

Changing of activity is what the market does best. It plays on your fears, emotions and desire to be a successful trader. It challenges your intelligence everyday. This is exactly why traders keep trying different methods and strategies as they watch their trading account shrink down to nothing.

The market changes everyday. It will not let any trader develop a consistently winning system.

To do so would cause its demise. Think about it for a minute. If it was just a matter of using some indicators, then every trader should be a winner. After all these years, traders would have figured out the best winning combination of indicators and every trader would make money everyday. If only trading life was that simple. But wait, for every winner there has to be a loser. Boy, that complicates things. Why can't we all win?

I warned you that you are trading against super computers and some very smart professional scammers, I mean traders. This is not just a game to them. They need to take your money to survive. You are not supposed to trade with any money that you cannot afford to lose. Therefore they do not feel guilty about taking it. And take it they do.

Do you really think that if you have one or two or twenty indicators that it will make a difference? Did you ever ask yourself why there are so many indicators? Does it make any sense? They keep inventing different ones because not a single one of them will work well enough to show consistent profits. If someone can make a line out of some obscure data and apply it to a chart, they will call it an indicator.

Only a fool would think they could jump in the market and beat the pros. Most day traders are fools in the sense that they are fooling themselves. Most lose all their money and quit within a year. A few more experienced traders are able stay in the game a little longer until they realize that they are just marks in a con game and will never be successful.

You had better be a strong trader right out of the gate if you want to hang around a while. Most traders are just beginners when they start trading. They lose their money very quickly and then quit. Most of the rest lose their money over time, and then quit. Either way, most day traders eventually quit.

You must understand, there are no guarantees in this game. The outside forces on this market are unpredictable. The odds are great against you that you will make it as a successful day trader. I am not saying that you can't be successful. I would never tell anyone that they could not accomplish any task that they aspire to perform.

My goal is just to make you aware that millions of day traders have already failed in what you are trying to do. They all failed for a reason. Maybe you think that you are smarter than all of them. If you do, then go for it.

You have to understand as a day trader that up is down and down is up at least half the time. The problem is that you never know when that is. How many times do we get bad news from the financial world and the stock market goes up instead of down? And vice verse.

News is also a big indicator that is used to make trading decisions. As a day trader watching the market very closely during the day, you need to know if any announcements are going to be made that day and know of any unpredictable fast breaking news that may impact your trading. The big problem is that by the time you get the news, the big institutions have already had the news and have taken positions.

And don't depend on the opening of the futures as an indicator to set the tone for the days trading. It could open down 150 points on bad news and end up 150 points for the day. News is breaking all the time that can potentially move the market. I can guarantee you one thing. You will not get it "before" the market makers.

You must remember that brokerage firms love the internet and being able to reach all the potential traders that are lining up worldwide. The Internet was the best thing for them since sliced bread (just an expression). Now, everyone in the world has access to the stock market game. They just have to play it up big and take all your commissions in the process. They really do not care if you win or lose, and don't think for a minute that they do. They make their money either way.

You cannot win at this game unless you know where price is going. That's it, PERIOD. Traders spend endless hours, days and years trying to figure it out watching charts. That's all they have to go on. They think just because it happened a certain way before, that it will happen that way again. And it will a percentage of the time, but you cannot trade it this way and be profitable. They spend endless amounts of money on trading systems that they believe will make them successful. They must wake from the nightmare.

Ever see an ad by a brokerage firm claiming that " 80% of our day-traders are winners"? Let's go a step further. Did you ever, in your life, see a brokerage firm claim any kind of general public day-trading success rate at all? Of course not because it does not happen. They offer a trading platform and hundreds of indicators and strategies but it is up to you, and you alone to outsmart the market and win.

In reality, they merely offer you a multitude of tools to analyze and make a trade decision. They would have you believe that they offer many different tools to help build your account. In reality they are tools to dismantle your account. They are like your local real estate broker who may sell the same house 5 or 10 times, and make a commission each time. Your brokerage firm will be more than happy to sell you the same stock or futures contract over and over again, and make a commission each and every time.

Your online brokerage firm will give you an elaborate trading platform, and all the fancy tools and indicators you can use to make your charts as fancy and colorful as you want. They want to make it as easy as possible for you to place your trades. You can easily place a trade from your laptop or even your smartphone in a matter of seconds. You can be assured that they will leave no stone unturned in order to separate you from your money.

Let it be known that I am not bashing online brokerage firms. I still use them for long-term trades. They provide a service that traders like and need. Online trading firms offer an easy way for mainstream traders to take part in the market without having to call a broker to place every trade.

Before online trading, it was almost impossible for the average trader to day trade in the manner that they do now with live data and charts. With a super fast Internet connection orders are matched at lightening speed so your execution takes place in less than a second. The whole concept is very exciting and challenging and it is very easy to get caught up in the action. It is just not profitable to most traders.

You will see many commercials and ads in publications by different trading companies, all wanting your business. The one thing that you will never see is an ad or commercial where they claim that they can make you profits on your trades. They will however give you the grandest illusion that you can make money if you do business with them because they offer everything you will need to succeed.

In summary, as fancy as they are, all indicators are lagging and cannot predict price movement with enough accuracy for you to be a successful day trader.

CHAPTER 6

TRADING SYSTEMS DEBUNKED

In this chapter we will look at just a few so called trading systems. There are literally thousands of trading systems out there and it is impossible to cover all of them. It really does not matter though because they all have one thing in common......they all lose money over time.

Most trading systems generally fall into a general trading category. So we will briefly look at a few categories that encompass most trading systems. Keep in mind that most trading systems are nothing more than a collection of indicators that line up for a trading signal. Most, if not all indicators print after price prints. Simply put, they are not psychic indicators in which they can predict the future of price with any certainty. They play the odds that what happened before, will happen again. You now have a 50-50 chance of a winning trade. You may as well just flip a coin or throw a dart. I know, they sure look good after the fact and all the backtesting. Try trading them for a yearly profit. Do you really think it would be that easy? Wouldn't all traders be winning? Yet, most are losers.

You have heard me make that point over and over again. That is because I want you to use common sense and think this through for yourself.

Don't ever fall for some so called trading expert willing to sell you his closely guarded trading secrets. It is inevitable that many new traders, some of professional intelligence, will fall for these schemes. They are so desperate to be successful that they are very vulnerable in their judgment. They do not want to be labeled a loser and they do not want to lose money. They falsely contend that the best way to win is from an "experienced trader" who "says" he is successful and has many trading "secrets" that he is willing to share with them. What do you think the chances are that they are simply a kind person willing to help other traders? If that was the case, why don't they do it for FREE?

I'm sorry; did I forget to mention that they are also willing to relieve you of several hundred or thousands of dollars for the privilege of knowing their secrets? There are no real successful trading secrets that the average trader will ever be privileged to know. Professional traders on the exchange floor and employed in big trading firms depend on us sheep for their profits and revenue stream. They have access to immediate information and "front run" most trades. How do you think they get those year-end bonuses?

There are just so many traders out there selling winning trading systems that it is hard to choose between them all. Yes, I am being facetious. Let me tell you a fact that you suspect but do not want to believe. Most of the time the only one winning is that person **selling** some kind of trading system, computer program or subscription service. They will try to convince you that they are making boatloads of money trading this system. Some are very professional in their delivery and web pages. Some will give you a trading history of "simulated trades", that always magically seem to produce profits all the time. I cannot stress enough this following point.

No single trading system works in all market conditions, and it never will.

How about this, tell them you do not care about their past trades either hypothetical (which most are) or real time. _**Tell them to show you their trading statements.**_ That's right, tell them to put up or shut up. This is where you separate the con artist liars from the legitimate traders. If they won't show you at least three years trading statements that prove their trading system performs as stated, they are hiding something. And that something is that they are trying to deceive you because they can't prove that their trading system is profitable. Ask them to show you their "actual annualized returns" over several different time periods, but don't get your hopes up.

For the sake of argument, even if you found one of those 10% of traders making a profit, chances of you being able to duplicate his success is a long shot. There are just to many variables and split second decisions needed in each trade.

Ever see those trading systems that advertise an 80% or 90% win rate? They are all over the place. Do you think they are lying to you? I'll let you figure that one out on your own, but let me ask you this question. If it was for real don't you think everyone would be trading it? There would be no losing traders and we would all be driving around in a Porsche and eating lobster. Use common sense and think it through.

Not only are there trading gurus touting their trading systems, there are companies touting their latest and greatest software. For just a few thousand dollars they promise to take you from novice to expert. If they are selling a system for thousands of dollars, they must be real professional traders right?

The fact is, they are professionals all right. But they are probably professional (or proficient) software developers, not traders. They developed some fancy way to show little green and red arrows and dots on the chart at some internal calculation.

Usually it is nothing more then some average crossover that lines up with another crossover. They will not show you the crosses so this is known as a "black box" computer program. You just get to see the "mysterious" colorful arrows or whatever else they dreamed up, as trade signals that pop up on your chart like magic. The more bells and whistles they include the better it looks to the trader who believes they have found something special that will give them an edge and make them a winner.

Don't be taken in by all the fancy graphics and directional arrows or months of data showing successful trades. Most, if not all, of these trades are "hypothetical". Which means that they never were taken in real time.

These trades were never taken as part of a "real trading study". They simply looked at historical data and decided where the trading system would have won. The entries and exits on these past trades are always judgmental and weighted heavily towards the developer so they show the most profit available. That's it in a nutshell, plain and simple. Almost every trading system was developed using some kind of historical data.

You see, that is all they have to go on. The simple premise that if it happened before, it will happen again. But as we know, history never repeats "exactly". Some little thing always changes. If the market was a constant then it would be predictable and the market could not exist. Think about that. It is always a guessing game because that is the way it has to be.

As I said before, it is impossible for me to review every day-trading system out there. But it does not really matter because they all have one common denominator.....they all lose eventually. But let's look at a couple of the most popular anyway.

Keep in mind that this is just a quick review to illustrate what trading these systems might look like on a daily basis. In reality they are much more intricate and complicated than what is discussed here. For those of you that have tried day trading these systems, you can identify with the comments. For the person who has not ever traded these systems, this is what you can expect. Also keep in mind that there are a multitude of different interpretations and variations of signals within each trading system. This of course makes them that much more difficult to trade successfully.

Any of these trading systems can be as simple or complicated as you want them to be. They are all open to the interpretation of the person who is using them.

THE NUMBER OF TRADING SYSTEMS OUT THERE AND THE CRITERIA IN WHICH THEY GIVE TRADING SIGNALS, IS ONLY LIMITTED BY THE IMAGINATION OF THE PERSON DEVELOPING THE SYSTEM

Did you ever hear of "Harmonic" trading? When you hear the word harmonic, you think music. Somebody slapped that word on to the way that chart patterns line up with Fibonacci numbers and came up with a fancy worded trading system called "Harmonic Trading". There are several different harmonic trading systems out there. Some actually encompass the ratios of music vibrations applied to charts. The main goal is to project price reversals. Just another attempt in the quest for that special magical indicator that does not exist.

Did you ever hear of "Market Profiling"? It is a completely different way of looking at price and charts. The chart is made up of alphabetical letters and prints Horizontally instead of up and down. They have terms like POC (point of control) and VA (value area) to make it interesting. This is just a different trading indicator derived from price and the end result is the same. Just because it is different does not make it better.

I will not even get into the way out there trading strategies that incorporate Astrology as a trading guide. That simply proves my point that traders will make a trading system out of just about anything.

So do you get the idea when it comes to the thousands of different trading systems out there? Let's look at the characteristics of some of these trading systems.

ELLIOTT WAVE

Lets, as an example, take any Elliott Wave Trading system for day trading. Lets say the 3 or 5-minute timeframe and chart. In order to understand this topic you should know a little about Elliott waves and how they are counted.

Elliott Wave is a great after the fact trading system, but almost impossible to day trade and very hard to trade in any time frame. RJ Elliott must have been an illusionist because EW analysis might show that you may have a particular wave count and then later (depending on your time frame) it changes and you don't see that wave count anymore. MOST TIMES THEY CHANGE AFTER YOU ENTER A TRADE, and your left holding a losing trade.

Elliott Waves are forever changing. It is good at giving several projections as to where a wave should end, but won't definitely confirm it ended until a previous wave high or low is broken by price. There are so many variables in

Elliott Wave that from a trading standpoint, it is impossible to be right and impossible to be wrong. Don't believe me, try day trading it. Of course one of the alternate counts are always right. If the original count turns out to be incorrect, there are always several more alternate counts. You can bet that the EW technician will fit one in there somehow, they always do.

Some technicians will tweak Elliott Wave and try to convince you that their way is much better because it is "different". I have seen Elliott Wave systems that use seven waves instead of five. I have seen EW systems that claim that there must be an ABC pattern in the fourth wave, where the "B" wave actually breaks the end of the 3rd wave. There are so many variations of Elliott Wave out there that it borders on ridiculous. Of course, most of them want you to buy this new trading wonder that will revolutionize day trading. But guess what, they still have several alternate counts anyways, so what good is it? No matter how you disguise it, if it walks like a duck and quacks like a duck......it's a duck.

Here is a typical example when using an EW computer trading program. If you are familiar with Elliott Wave, you should be able to follow along. Let's say some Elliott Wave computer trading system tells you that you are most likely at the end of a wave 2 up, and gives you a potential short signal. It is telling you that price has met one of the wave 2 retracement areas. These are usually some Fibonacci number, although Elliott Wave analysis does have its own set of rules. Let's say it is a 38% price retrace.

Now remember, and this is very important. This potential wave 2 has NOT been confirmed yet by any Elliott Wave count. This is simply a "projection". It is simply telling you that "if this is the right count and you enter a trade here, you can expect to take profits there". You are expecting a wave 3 down. You know that wave 3's are usually the longest and most profitable, so you hope for a nice drop and profit gain. You take the short signal with the usual stop above the wave 2 high. The market doesn't see it your way and stops you out for a loss. Wave 2 is what is called "extending".

Let's say this price retrace went to about 55%. To no one's surprise the Elliott Wave count was wrong. The actual first count is wrong about 70% of the time, according to my experience. Now, here is the kicker. If you go back to your computer program and run the analysis again, chances are that the count and trade you just lost on have completely "disappeared". Like it was never there. Now a new count is in play. Doesn't help you any because you just lost money.

Let's continue. Let's say, you get another signal telling you that you are at the end of wave 2 down. Price is at the 38% retrace area. You remember that the last time you entered at the 38% area you got burned with a loss, so you figure that you will wait for the 50% area this time. But price never retraces that far and heads up in a massive wave 3, without you. You see, it is always a guessing game. I use the computer program as an example but the same holds true for those EW technicians doing it on a chart.

Now, you might think that this is not a losing trade for you, but guess what, you lost money by not taking it. Nothing may have come out of your account, but it was a losing trade just the same. This is where most traders get it wrong. You cannot afford to miss those winning trades. **You will find that you will miss many winning trades, but you will never miss a losing trade.**

Remember we are on the short 3 or 5-minute time frame. Larger time frames will incur larger losses. It is very common to have several losing trades in a row with Elliott Wave trading. With a 70% + loss ratio, it is not uncommon to have 7+ losers in a row (if you are taking all signals). How many traders can take that many losses in a row?

Elliott Wave Theorists like to think of Elliott Wave as a leading indicator instead of just another old lagging indicator. Do not be fooled. It is nothing more than a "guessing" indicator that constantly changes. There is always the "if" factor. If this count is in play, then this scenario could happen. If that's not the count, then maybe this is the "alternate" count and this scenario could happen.

This can and does repeat for as many alternate counts as the technician needs to make it so they are right.

Did you ever try counting the waves in Elliott Wave Theory? Do you really think it is so easy as five waves up in an impulse wave followed by three waves down in a corrective wave? Pick any timeframe and try counting them. If it was that clear-cut and easy, then everyone would be trading millionaires. How many do you know?

In reality there are all kinds of extra waves that can be thrown in the count. There can be many sub-waves in a count. These are waves that sub-divide into smaller waves and are used when the original count is extending. There can also be what seems like an endless number of A and B waves in a count. That is all the chartist can do when the count does not do what it was supposed to do. There can be several Fibonacci "extensions" to a wave if it does not stop where it is supposed to. There can be several "X" waves thrown in to a count if the market stays sideways. That is an extra wave thrown in there when the preferred count is not working out. There are "flats" and "diagonals" and all kinds of neat things that they use to make the count the way they like it. Elliott Wave is never wrong, after the fact. They simply keep changing the count until it is right. This tactic is the same for short or long time frame counts.

Most of the Elliott Wave trading systems have many losing trades and would have you believe that if you take all those losers, eventually, a winner will come along and if you let it run, you will make back all your losses and turn a profit. Now, there is no guarantee how big that winner will be (how long a price run). There is also no guarantee you will take the trade. And there is no guarantee that you will get maximum profits from the trade. Almost all traders take profits early. They are afraid of losing profits made and are easily shaken from the market.

The point is this. No matter what a developer claims about a trading system (any trading system) on his website, chances are that most, if not all, will lose money trading it. They will try their best to have you believe that it is YOUR fault that you are losing money. You are not trading the system right. You are not taking the right trades or you must hold through the drawdowns and let the winners run. Do not believe them. The fact is that ten traders will trade the system and signals ten different ways and get ten different results. This is "human " nature.

NOTE: All trading systems have what they refer to as "Draw Downs". This is when a particular trading system goes through a period of time and does not seem to work. The trading signals look great, just like they always did, but the market does not do what it is supposed to do. This leads to many losing trades and loss of trading capital.

There are so many Elliott Wave Technicians out there that the more prominent ones "add" their own little adjustments. There are so many variations it makes ones head spin. We talk about Elliott Wave for day trading here, but it works equally as "bad" for longer time frames. They are always adjusting to make a count fit in there somewhere. Some of the more well known ones who are almost never right (no names here) make one single lucky call in their life and are followed blindly thereafter by thousands of traders.

The fact is, a day trader has to make many correct decisions for a trade to be successful. The chances of you making more good ones than bad ones on a consistent basis are not good odds. Make just one mistake and you lose the trade. As a day trader, you already are picking the most volatile trading vehicles to trade because you need price movement. You are trying to hit a moving target every day. This in itself increases risk. At least the buy and hold investors and long term swing traders have an advantage in this regard.

TREND DAY TRADING SYSTEMS

Another popular way to trade is with Trend Following Systems. Ever hear the slogan "the trend is your friend"? Well, for longer term traders this may be true, but in day trading the trends are volatile and can turn on a dime. Let's face it, in a bull market, you could buy just about any general mutual fund and it will go up. Notice I did not say sector funds, as these rotate in cycles and do not always

75

follow the market. Also, I did not say all stocks because picking winning stocks takes time and research.

You can trade an index ETF or option in a bull market trend and have a reasonable chance to make a profit if you hold it long enough. And here in lies the problem. For most investors and traders it all comes down to time frames and how long you can hold the position before being shaken out by the market. Day trading timeframes are the most volatile.

In order to obtain a trend in any timeframe, price has to print on the chart. On a 333-tick chart, it may only take a few minutes to define a trend. But if you look at a five-minute chart, it may take twenty minutes to define a trend. It does not matter what time frame you use, a trend will only tell you where price has been, not where it is going.

Once again, we are looking back at price and somehow think we know where price will head. We are just assuming that price will continue in the trend direction. But a trend has to end at some point, and those points are not very predictable. Here is where all those indicators that are only right 50% of the time come in to play as they cross over at some point and give a trading signal. The idea is to enter a new trend change at the beginning and ride it for profits. Seems simple enough, but just never seems to work out that way for consistent profits. There are to many false signals.

As a very quick typical example, price has been trending up all morning and you want to catch some of the big move. You do not want to get left behind, so you enter a trade long because your indicator crossed. But you happen to enter during a price run, that turns out to be the END of the run. Wow, how are you supposed to know when a price run will end? In other words, it is impossible to know for sure when a trend will end. They can turn on a dime or continue farther than anyone would have thought.

Remember back in our brief discussion about Elliott Waves, a price run is defined as a wave of some degree. So price reverses and begins to go against you almost immediately after you enter the trade. You are now losing money. You do not know if it is just a price pullback or the start of a new trend in the opposite direction. Do you sell?

Most traders do not like to lose money immediately after initiating a position. But this is what will happen if you get caught in a price retrace. Then you start to think about how far it will pull back and how much money you will lose. The market is an expert at playing mind games with you. You think that maybe the market is about to turn over so you panic and exit your position for a loss. After a period of price chop, the price reverses and starts to go up again. So to quickly recap, yes you entered long in a trend and yes you lost money. So...was the trend your friend?

Trend systems will work fine on those few trending days a month. All you have to do is make sure you win more on those days than you lose the rest of the month. Oh yes, also you must ride those winning days until the very end and for all they are worth. And last but not least, they must be big trends with enough points available to offset all the losses in between these trend days. More time than not, most of the big move happens in the overnight session....while you are sleeping. They just shut you out or limit any profits that you could make.

This was just one simple example. So even in an up trend, no one knows when it will end and turn around. Each retrace of price could be the start of the BIG drop. Sometimes price retraces in a strong trend are nothing more than areas of profit taking. But how can you tell the difference between a price retrace and a possible market turn? You cannot. The market will repeat this maneuver over and over as traders get stopped out for losses along the way. That is the job of the market...to keep you confused.

A confused trader is a losing trader. An average trader can only take so much mental stress. How many people do you know who sold at or near the bottom of the 2008 - 2009 market drop? Once the selling programs on all those super computers kicked in, it was an avalanche in the making. Most of those that panicked as they watched their IRA lose massive amounts of money, never re-entered the market to catch the move up to get their money back. Many swore they would never invest in the stock market again.

Just to show you the market doesn't care who's money it takes, most of these were longer-term investors in IRA's and 401k's and not day traders. You see, day traders get spanked on a daily basis. But every so often long-term investors get a little taste of what it feels like to be a day trader.

Remember the markets primary function is to take your money. It is after all just a game. A manipulated game. I cannot stress this enough and I repeat it over and over. That small minority of successful day traders that are on the exchange floors or work for big trading firms need your money to survive.

They have on their side, all the online trading firms advertising their latest and greatest trading innovations to get you to think you can beat the market. Most of them have apps that allow you to trade from your smartphone. You can virtually trade from anywhere.

Many day traders will place their trades using a short time frame but base their trend trades in the direction of a longer time frame. If they trade on the one-minute chart, they may only trade in the direction of the 5-minute chart trend. This may seem safe in theory, but the fact is that no one knows when the trend will change and you will still get whipsawed in the shorter time frame.

Here is another common scenario. Price will move fast right after the open. Traders are not in the market yet as they wait to see what the trend will be for the day. Most missed the big move. Price will flatten out and traders will place their trades as they guess which way price will go. Price will move up and down for a while, stopping longs and shorts out in the price chop and fake outs. When most of the traders have quit for the day, price will move again in the last hour or so, in the direction they want to take it. They do not want you to make any money on any of the price movement.

If you are thinking that you can easily identify either of these two trading scenarios when they occur, you are mistaken. They are only easily identified *after* the trading day. These are just two of the many trading scenarios the market uses to keep traders off guard. It is a guessing game every day.

Trend trading is simply trading with the trend. It can be as simple or complicated as the trader wants it to be. Which trend and on what time frame is up to the trader. Trading with the trend will not guarantee you winning trades on the short day trading time frames.

I am not giving financial advice but trading longer term with the trend can be profitable and less risky if done with caution.

BREAKOUT TRADING SYSTEMS

Another popular trading system would be the "Breakout" strategy. This is simply initiating a strategy where you place a buy order above the current price and a sell order below the current price. After some moving average or macd line crossover this is probably the next most popular way to trade. These types of trades are usually done on Index contracts and individual stocks.

Here is a simple example. Let's say the ES (SP emini futures contract) was trading between 1398 and 1400 and was stalled there for a short while. This is commonly referred to as "congestion". You know price will not stay in between those numbers for long. You would put an order in to buy above the 1400 price thinking that if price broke out higher that it would continue up and you would ride the trend for a profit. You would also put an order to sell below the 1398 price with the expectation that if price broke out lower, it would continue in a downtrend. This is break out trading. Remember the smaller the time frame, the smaller the risk (because your stops are usually closer), but also the smaller the profit expectation.

As far as picking or choosing the numbers that you enter a trade at, they are usually above and below the prices of congestion. That is what every other trader is doing, and we want to be just like them right? WRONG!

There are also other ways to trade breakouts. If you want to get more technical you can incorporate buying or selling if a certain time bar is breached or if a high or low is breached after say 10:30 est. The time 10:30 is a magic number, just ask any emini trader. There are many systems just based on this time. Some systems go long if the first hour high is breached and go short if the first hour low is breached. Other trading systems do just the opposite.

Now, here is the thing. You will get faked out and stopped out, much more often than being on the correct side of the trade and able to ride a trend for a profit. And by profit, I mean being able to make up for all the losses you incur by being whipsawed and stopped out on previous trades using this method.

Many breakout trading systems are designed around a news event. The most popular event is when the FOMC (Federal Open Market Committee) meets and discusses monetary policy. The FOMC meets 8 times each year. Usually at around 2:00pm EST, they will release their minutes and any decision that was made.

The stock market is usually flat in anticipation of any breaking news. Once the news is released, the stock market usually picks up in volatility. There can be large price spikes after an announcement. Traders of breakout trading systems do not care which way price breaks out as they have entry prices on both the long and short sides.

I know what you are thinking. This seems like a perfect trading system where the trader cannot lose. How could they because they are covered both ways? But let's dig into this perfect system a little further.

In most instances the market will spike wildly in both directions. More time than not, it will get you in a trade and then reverse to stop you out. At this point, price is moving very fast. If you get back in a trade in the opposite direction, the market has a tendency to reverse and stop you out again. The market may repeat these swings several times before moving in a specific direction.

Also, if your buy and sell entry points are to close together, a wild swinging fast market can get you into both trades within seconds unless you are using an OCO order (one cancels the other). It is not unusual for price on the indexes to swing several points within mere seconds after an FOMC announcement.

Most times, you as a trader will get whipsawed and lose money. Your position may initially show a small profit but unless you can see the future, you have absolutely no clue where to exit your trade. Your first inclination is to hold for a nice profit.

These types of trading systems involve placing a trade once price has moved above or below a certain point. For whatever reason, the trader expects the price of the Index to continue in that direction far enough for them to make a profit. Usually price would be breaking through a support or resistance level. However it could be any level that the trader has come up by using any number of trading indicators.

My experience with this type of trading is that you will get whipsawed into poverty. The market will get you in a trade and stop you out almost like it knows exactly where your entry and stop numbers were placed.

I don't care what you use for criteria, the end results are always the same. Many shysters have made themselves wealthy by selling these types of trading systems. I have seen them for thousands of dollars, being promoted by fancy videos from exotic tropical places and live trading seminars. They want to glorify the feeling of a carefree life style that can be yours if you just buy their trading system. You can be sipping Margaritas by the pool like them if you had their trading system. This is just another of many illusions that you will see.

They will inform you that there are only 250 trading systems available and you better hurry if you want one. They then spam your email box for the next week, letting you know that the number of available systems is dropping down and you better hurry. There are only 120 left. There are only 75 left. They will tell you that once these 250 systems are sold, that they will never be available again to the public. After all, they do not want to saturate the world with to many winning trading systems.

Just Google or YouTube "breakout day-trading systems". Hundreds of videos and systems complete with all the charts, bells & whistles, and proof you need to plunk down your hard earned money and buy one. And every one of them a winning system with their own special name. How about that!! A smorgasbord of stock and emini trading systems that will allow you to trade for a living and promise to make you wealthy. This in itself would raise the red flag to anyone with any common sense at all. But once we get it in our head to try day trading, nothing or no one is going to stop us. We just have to give it a shot.

I am trying to give you a heads up and hope I can help a few traders save their money. Invest in mutual funds or buy and hold stocks for the longer term. Swing trading on a longer time frame will satisfy your trading appetite and also give you a slightly better chance to win. Just do not day trade.

Do not believe anything you see or read about traders sharing their newly discovered winning trading system with you. How about a short lesson in Psychology. We humans are by nature, a violent species. Has there ever been a time where there was not a war going on somewhere?

That is why we as the human race need laws, to protect us from each other. This is very sad but true.

It is also human nature to keep a "good thing" a secret. If you truly had a winning trading system that could make you wealthy, there is no way you would share it with the public. You might keep it in the family so everyone close to you may prosper, but you would not share it with your competitors. To do so would jeopardize your success. Once it is out for the public to trade, it will no longer be profitable, if it ever was at all.

So do you begin to see the problem here with all these winning systems? Yes, there are many times that these trading systems will produce winning trades and profits. But here is that pesky word again, "consistent". They are not consistent enough to make you a profitable day trader.

COUNTER TREND DAY TRADING SYSTEMS

Some of the most popular day-trading systems are COUNTER TREND SYSTEMS. The most popular include systems that signal trades at Fibonacci retrace percentages, some indicator divergence with price, high volume bars on big price moves, Elliott Wave corrective waves, support and resistance level areas, and double price tops and bottoms. There are many others, but these are the ones that are traded the most.

You have heard the terms " step in front of a moving train" or "catch a falling knife". Well, this is what you do when you try to counter trade. Yes, you guessed it. The results are not pleasant.

More often than not you get run over, chopped up and are stopped out for a loss. The theory is that after any run in price there will be a price retracement also known as a correction. This makes sense because we know that price can not run in one direction forever. So now it turns into a guessing game by counter trend traders as to when price will reverse.

Now, let's look at Fibonacci numbers as an example because they are the one trading indicator looked at by most traders whether they trade it or not. It is the universal reference indicator. There are several Fibonacci retracement numbers. They are 23.6%, 38.2%, 50% and 61.8%. Price is supposed to retrace to any one of these numbers and then magically reverse and continue in the direction of the first trend. Theoretically, if price retraces past 61.8%, then the trend will change and continue in that direction. Doesn't always happen, just sometimes, like everything else in this game.

The problem here is that you do not know which number to pick to enter a trade. You really never know where or if price will reverse at any of these numbers. You could conceivably have four losing trades in a row if you tried to enter on each retrace number because price will many times retrace all of the run and then some. You just do not know. They are not reliable enough to be consistently profitable.

Here is an example of what happens during a typical trade using Fibonacci numbers. Let's say that you were trading a 3- minute chart and price has just completed a 6 point run up and stalled. The market pulled back and price retraced to the 38.2% area and stalled there giving you the impression that it will reverse and continue up. So you enter a trade long with a stop below the low of the retrace. Price then continues to retrace and stops you out of your trade. Price then pulls back to the 50% retracement level and stalls again. Not wanting to miss the trade, you take a position long again with a stop below the last price low of the pullback. Price meanders around in this area and stops you out again after price retraced 54%. Price does not know it was supposed to stop at the 50% retracement level. You are now waiting for the next Fibonacci retracement level which would be 61.8%, but price reverses and takes off without you in the same direction that you were just in on two previous trades.

Another counter-trend strategy would be large exhaustion bars. These are very long Extended Vertical Reversal Bars signifying the termination of a price run. They are supposed to signal a price reversal when the close of the bar is in the 30% range of the start of the bar. A long extended price bar at the end of a price run in the up direction is climatic buying exhausting itself. A long extended price bar at the end of a price run in the down direction is climatic selling exhausting itself. They work about 50% of the time, just like everything else.

Many day traders watch certain indicators like the TRIN or TICK for possible price reversals in a trend. A tick chart draws a new price bar after a certain number of "ticks" specified by the trader and does not care about "time". A tick equals one trade. The theory is that when the tick volume picks up the price bars print very fast and signify professional buying or selling at the end of a price run. A trader would want to look for a reversal trade after this type of action. You will find that they are confusing and ambiguous to say the least and are wrong as much as they are right. There are also floor trader PIVOTS that every trader in the world watches. They are practically useless for trading. There are numerous indicators like Bollinger Bands, double tops or bottoms in price and candlestick patterns that all are interpreted as counter trade signals. The results are almost always the same. Not good for your trading account.

As I stated before, it is impossible to review every counter trend day trading system or indicator available on the market. One fact I can guarantee you is that any winning trading system is only temporary. Sooner or later the market will change its characteristics and that winning system will start to lose. It is possible and likely that you will lose all the profits that you made and then some.

SCALPING DAY TRADING SYSTEMS

These are very fast moving trading systems. These trades are mostly done on the index contracts, but can be done with stocks also. These indexes include the S&P 500, Russell, and Dow Jones. Most index trades placed are of emini variety.

Those traders scalping stocks are usually looking for .10 to .15 cents profit per share. You will need to trade 1000 shares of a stock to make $100 if you are taking .10 cents a share. If the stock sells for $20.00 per share, you will need $20,000 in your account to place this trade. If you have a margin account, you may need only half that amount depending on your brokerage firm. Most stock scalpers make several trades in a day and are almost always considered pattern day traders. In this case they would need to maintain $25,000 in their trading account.

These trades are all placed electronically as fast as your Internet connection will get it there. These are usually done on shorter time frames ranging from the "tick" increment to the 5-minute time frame. These are the most popular because a day trader needs price volatility in order to develop many trade setups.

This method of day trading was not possible from home or office until the roll out of high-speed Internet connections. It opened up a brand new gigantic pool from which to pull money, the average home trader.

For explanation purposes lets use the S&P 500 eminis as an example. Institutional Traders who are scalpers just want a very small move in the underlying index to make a profit. They make take profits on increments as low as .25 (one quarter) of a point and make a profit by trading hundreds of contracts. Most home scalpers take from between one and two points on the emini because they are only trading from one to five contracts. Scalpers will miss every nice price run because they do not let their trades run with profits. They are just looking for crumbs. You will have to calculate commissions on each trade because that could diminish much of your profits.

Scalpers can have many round turn trades in a daily trading session. Initially it looks easy. How hard could it possibly be to just guess price direction and get just one point? Thousands have tried it and failed.

Lets break down a trader scalping one point profit on the ES (S&P emini) and losing one point stop loss on each trade. If they win 5 trades and lose 5 trades, you would think that they broke even. This is not correct as they paid commissions on 10 round turn trades.

The fees vary from broker to broker but an average would be between $5.00 and $7.00 round turn per contract. Let's use the mid price of $6.00 per contract. If that trader was trading at least two contracts, they **_lost_** :

10 trades x 2 contracts x $6/per contract = $120.00 They won half their trades but still lost money.

If the trader won six of the ten trades they would only make $80 for their trouble. It breaks down like this:

Six wins ($600 profit) - Four losses ($400) - $120 commissions = $80 net profit. Let me say that to win six of ten trades consistently is very difficult to accomplish. There is no room for mistakes in judgment or emotions and most traders simply cannot do it. All that time wasted for just $80 in profit. Are you kidding me?

These are fast moving trades and many of them depend on a moving average line of some type of indicator crossing over another average line. A cross in the down direction would indicate a "sell" signal and a cross in the up direction would indicate a "buy" signal. The action is fast and a trader must be able to take all the current market action as input, compute the data in your brain, and make lightening fast "correct" decisions. All that stress and anguish for playing a game that you only have a very slim chance to win.

The simple crossing indicators are the most common but any indicator of preference can be used. Many scalpers think they have an advantage by using "price bars" as their signal. They think that since price does not lag like indicators, they are in a better position to make profits if they can just figure out a winning strategy. They revert to candlestick charting to take advantage of all the various configurations. They have some fancy names like dojis, hammers, dark clouds, hanging man, morning star and more. They are not reliable enough to trade profitably. They are just another visual way to look at the market. It is just another illusion.

In reality, I know many traders that delved into these markets with sure fire trading systems and lost all their capital in a very short time. Would you try to fly a jumbo jet without fully understanding what every instrument meant? Then why would you try to trade a market without a full understanding of how it worked?

Scalping is very hard on your emotions and nerves. Scalping will take your stress level up and your health and trading account down. At some point you will lose control and "chase" the market on impulse and it will not end well as the losses mount up. You can easily wipe out many weeks of profit in a single day. You are after all, a human being.

OPTIONS AND SPREADS

This section references most index options but the same holds true for most stock options also. The difference being that the index options are much more volatile and prone to a multitude of news events worldwide, where the individual stock option has a different set of criteria that moves it. Sometimes an individual stock will move in the complete opposite direction of the general stock market. Options are popular because of the leverage they have. As an example, one option contract is equivalent to 100 shares of stock. The cost of the stock option is only a fraction of what it would cost to purchase the 100 shares, but you would still control 100 shares and take profits and losses accordingly.

Options can be very simple or very complicated and one must know what they are doing if they are going to trade these financial vehicles. A trader can lose a lot of money very fast if they do not fully understand the strategy they implemented. There are hundreds if not thousands of books written on this subject. The purpose of this section is to give you some general facts and substance to think about. You should be able to figure out on your own that most option trades do not end well. We will not discuss the endless option strategies or the many different ways for you to combine and trade option contracts. We will pick a few of the more popular option trades and analyze how they most often play out.

You have probably heard the expression that about 90 percent of options expire worthless. Well, that could be a good thing or a bad thing depending on whether you bought the option or sold the option. That is why options are so confusing and the CBOE does a good job of keeping them that way while giving the ILLUSION that most traders are making money. According to the CBOE, that is statistically not a true statement. They estimate that only about 30% of options actually expire worthless. They go on to claim that only 10% of options are exercised in each month and that 60% of options are closed usually in the week before expiration. They do not state if they were closed for a profit or a loss because they have no way of knowing if the options were combined with different trading strategies. They also do not want you to know that most of them were for losses. If you read between the lines you can see that

90% of the options are not exercised, but this does not mean they expired worthless. This also does not mean that the options were profitable.

There have been some studies made on the profitability of options for the average trader. They have found that retail (not institutional) options traders have lost an average of about 5% of their trading account each month. Now to put it into perspective, it is important to remember that most traders will only risk about 5 to 10 percent of their account each month. Clear it up any?

It is not always a steady decline of your trading account. You might win one or two months and lose the next three, or any other combination to fall into the average. I know some traders that consider themselves successful if they just break even at the end of the year. For some reason that eludes me, they think that they beat the market. Obviously they do not depend on their trading skills to eat or pay all their bills. I consider it a totally wasted year and waste of precious time that could be spent golfing.

Let's analyze some details of trading options. The most popular method of trading options is just to "buy" or "sell" them. If you just simply buy or sell option contracts you must be right in your direction and time frame. If you "buy" a "call" option, you are betting the stock or market is going to move up within a certain time frame to win the trade. But if the market or stock moves down, moves up to slow or stays sideways, then you lose the premium you paid. You win one out of four scenarios. That's only a 25% chance of winning. If you went into surgery with a 25% chance of surviving, would you think that that is a good thing? The same holds true if you "buy" a "put" option contract. Now if you are psychic and have a crystal ball then never mind.

Here is one pitch you will come across eventually. They want to sell you an option program that includes spreads in which you can make a steady 1-3% weekly profit or 10% monthly profit. This usually is initiating an "Iron Condor" spread strategy if you are trading the monthly contracts. This strategy is almost the opposite of the above simple buy or sell strategy. With this strategy you want the strike price to stay within the parameters of your spread for the allotted time. Usually you are putting this traded on with the price in the middle of your parameters, and you want price to stay there. Since you sold the spread, that means you received a premium that you want to keep. If the price moves beyond the parameters of your spread, in either direction, then you lose a lot of money very fast. So, you want a slow moving or stagnate price movement for your option to expire worthless in which case you keep the premium in your trading account.

Here are the scenarios you will see most often. Price will move against you quickly and force you to extend your parameters or close the trade for a loss. Price will move against you slowly and force you to extend your parameters or close the trade for a loss. When you extend your parameters you incur expenses and your profit margin shrinks or disappears. At this point you are just trying to get out of the trade without losing to much money. Price will move rather quickly in your direction and force you to extend your parameters or close the trade for a loss. Price will move slowly in your direction and in the last week before option expiration force you to move your parameters or close the trade for a loss. There is only one scenario in which you can win. That is for price to remain inside your strike price parameters.

The same strategy is used for the weekly contracts but "Bull Puts" and "Bear Calls" are favored because of the shorter time frame. The idea is to sell contracts so far out of the money that they almost always expire worthless. The phrase "almost always" should get your attention. First, there is a considerable amount of work that you must do and be responsible for. You must pick the stock or index you want to trade and then pick your strike prices and time frame for executing the trade. This is all on you so you better be good at reading charts, technical analysis, world news and overall guessing (which is the most important). What could go wrong?

With these types of trading, there will be several winning weeks or months in a row. But eventually, along will come a losing month or two and put you right back where you started. Another problem is that if they do expire worthless and you keep the small premium and pay commissions, it just is not worth the time to a trader looking to make serious money. This is especially true of the weekly option spreads where your profit margins are very small .The person selling the trading strategy gives the illusion that if you buy his CD or Video disks that you will have a money machine giving you guaranteed profits every week or month. This simply is not the case for most traders.

Trading the index options are much more risky than trading the stock options because the market can swing violently in either direction at any time. Even if you are an experienced chartist and technical analyst, you are still at the mercy of the manipulated market makers. On top of that, any worldwide news event can move the stock market up or down very fast and without any warning.

CHAPTER 7

ONLINE SEMINARS AND VIDEOS

These are probably the most powerful trading sales technique there are. There is absolutely nothing more convincing than watching someone make a trade and profits right in front of you. Most of these videos are done on a trading simulator and there is absolutely no risk of them losing any money. The seller of a trading system simply keeps taping videos until one works out to be a winner. They then tweak the sales pitch as they talk, and add graphics, bells and whistles so it looks professional. Then they post it on their website or upload it to You Tube for any vulnerable trader to view. You watch the video, they win and it directs you to their website.

Once on their website, there will be additional videos of all winning trades as well as a history of winning trades. Usually they post by the month. So within that month you would have many winners and a few losers (even they aren't stupid enough to pass the system off as ALL winners). One thing for sure is that at the end of a high majority of months, they end with big profits. And the one or two losing months end with just a very small loss. This is done by design.

Now they got your attention. They just need to set the hook and reel you in. To do this they promote some "limited time special offer", because they do not want you to think about it to long. You might come to your senses and talk yourself out of it. They may even offer a "guarantee" for a specified number of days. This is your RED FLAG. Run far away. Nobody can guarantee you any profits in the stock market. How can they when they do not know what the market is going to do next.

Now, here is the kicker on those guarantees. If you lose money, which you probably will, you must send them a list of your trades to analyze. Almost always it will be your fault that you lost because you took a trade you should not have. They will find a reason not to refund your money as they promised.

They will have you believe that you made a crucial mistake in your judgment and interpretation of the trading system. It will always be this way because they have no intentions of ever refunding any money to purchasers of their system. Smart ones may refund one or two a year just in case they are audited by the SEC, due to many complaints. But most times, the trader will just feel humiliated because he is portrayed at not being smart enough to win, and just never trade the system again. They are counting on you to be ashamed that you cannot win, and just go away.

I lost track at how many online seminars and videos I have watched throughout my trading career. I especially like the "live " seminars. You know the ones. You get emails notifying you of winning trades with this special system, and an up coming live day trading seminar. You get two or three weeks of so called winning trades just to pump you up and get you excited. Now remember, just because it is a live trading seminar does not mean that he is trading a live account. More than likely, he is trading on a simulator. One way you may tell is if he is getting filled by just "touching" the price, it is most likely a simulator. Most trading platforms will not guarantee you an entry fill until price trades through your set price.

Let's say the big day arrives and you are watching the live trading seminar. If they have a winning trade, you will be given a chance to order this trading system right now. They will inform you that they only have a certain number to sell and that you better hurry. If you do not buy that day, you will receive emails every day informing you that there are only a few left and you may miss out on a trading opportunity of a lifetime if you do not buy today. It is human nature to want or possess something special that no one else or very few have. It is also human nature to never want to miss an opportunity. The seller of the system is aware of these tendencies and will stop at nothing to get you to make an irrational decision.

Just to put this in perspective. Let's say the con artist, I mean seller, has 1000 viewers all over the world. Let's say that 20% (200) buy the system for $1000. The seller walks away with $200,000 cash in his bank account. I personally know of traders that did this very thing. The price of $1000 is a price that new and desperate traders seem willing to part with. Anything more than that, you are targeting a more affluent clientele.

If they lose during the live trade seminar, they simply point out that not every trade can possibly be a winner. That is how it is in trading. They will bring your attention to the several weeks of winning trades that they sent you in your email. They will still put the system up for sale with the same hype as if they had just won the live trade. Their goal is to make you rush to purchase their trading system before it is "sold" out. They want you to make an impulsive decision to buy right on the spot. They do not want to give you time to think about it and come to your senses.

There are also "live" seminars that you must physically attend. It is usually hosted by some "successful" trader of some "special" trading system. It is almost always some setup of price formation and they give it some fancy name. And oh yes, I almost forgot. They charge you a hefty price to attend and they almost always have something to sell you. Some times it is a trading course and sometimes it is a book.

Let me ask you a question. If a billionaire like Bill Gates puts on a seminar about starting a company and becoming wealthy, and 1000 people attend, do you think they <u>all</u> will become billionaires? My guess is that not even one person will become a billionaire. There was a lot of luck involved in the OS (operating system) chosen to be the standard at the time. It could have just as easily gone to IBM. So why would you attend a day trading seminar and think you can be just like him or her? Because they said so?

How about all those "Real Estate" seminars that show you how to become wealthy by investing in property. All you have to do is buy a condo and rent it out or buy a house and sell it for more that you paid for it. Sounds simple enough. So, do you think all the attendees of the real estate seminar will become wealthy like the person giving it? Absolutely not. It all comes down to geographical location and what cycle the real estate market is in. Timing and location is everything when dealing with real estate, just ask all the people who went under water in their home loans during the last housing bubble in the U.S.

How about this one. How many times have you seen a multi-time lottery winner do an interview on television about how to win the lottery? Do you really think that if you do what he says that you to will win the lottery? Do you think everyone watching won the lottery? He was lucky. There are lucky traders also, but there is a far greater amount of losers, just like the lottery.

We would like to believe that we could achieve the same success that the person doing the seminar had. The fact is, many conditions, some beyond their control, worked in their favor for them to succeed. They are the exception, not the norm.

CHAPTER 8

SUMMARY

I have laid out my case as to why you should take a long hard realistic look at day trading or even short term swing trading. I have given many personal and general experiences that I hope expose day trading as the losing game that it is. I have shown facts and figures that day trading is a losing proposition to about 90% of the day traders. This is a fact whether you accept it or not.

I understand that it is extremely difficult to persuade someone not to try something that they are convinced they can win at. If you do decide to day trade, it is important that you realize what you are up against. The purpose of this book is to open your eyes to the side of day trading that most of the traders will see. What you do with this information is up to you. If you have fifteen or twenty thousand dollars that you don't mind losing by day trading the stock market, then by all means have fun. But if you enter the stock market expecting to trade for a living or turn that twenty thousand dollars into a small fortune, you are looking at an Illusion. Just like the Illusionists make buildings disappear, the trading establishment will make your money disappear.

Like any book, I am sure this book will have its critics. That's just the way life is. There will be those that say that the author could not make it day trading so he wrote a book to bash day trading. They will say that he am a sore loser and has a chip on his shoulder. The facts are that I day traded professionally for five years initiating from one to six trades a day and still managed to hang around with the initial trading account. This is a feat in itself. I have had access to hundreds of day traders and I can tell you that the facts do not lie. I did not write this book to bash day traders, I wrote this book to help day traders make an informed decision by showing them how the illusion works. Do you believe in magic?

The trading industry has safer methods for you to participate in the stock market if that is where you want to invest your money. If you want to put money in the stock market, then do so on a longer timeframe in general market growth mutual funds or dividend paying Blue Chip stocks. Be an investor and not a trader. The stock market, on average, has one down year for every four up years. Using this logic, you will always eventually make money in the long term. Yes, there will be declines, but although there are no guarantees, the market has always come back through history. Always invest according to your risk tolerance and timeframe. If you do not want to actively follow the stock market then hire a financial planner to do it for you. I wish you the best no matter what you decide.

Ken Bednar

ABOUT THE AUTHOR

Ken holds Degrees in Business Management and Electrical Engineering. He has traded in the stock market for over 25 years while he worked and raised a family. After Ken retired he day traded professionally for 5 years.

During his trading career he has witnessed the internet revolution and dangerous day trading frenzy. Ken continues to trade in the stock market but on a much longer time frame than day trading.